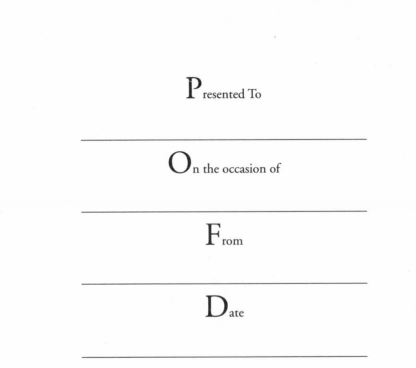

Presented To

_____

On the occasion of

_____

From

_____

Date

_____

POWER
IN HIS
NAME

The Wonderful Names of Our Wonderful Lord

A Barbour Book

ecpa Member of the
Evangelical Christian
Publishers Association

Published by   Barbour and Company, Inc.
                P.O. Box 719
                Uhrichsville, Ohio 44683

Printed in the United States of America

A Star and a Sceptre

"…I shall see him, but not now: I shall behold him, but not nigh; there shall come a Star out of Jacob, and a Sceptre shall rise out of Israel…." NUMBERS 24:17

What could be more beautiful or more fitting than that our Lord should be called a Star? Those who know Him best may say, "I shall see Him, but not now. I shall behold Him, but not nigh." But all the world shall know that Jesus is also a sceptre that shall rise out of Israel. Evil will be destroyed before His righteousness more swiftly than ice must melt before the glowing sun. From far beyond our world of trouble and care and change, Jesus in His glorious holiness shines with undimmed light, offering to all who will follow Him, the promise of a better day.

Lord, lead us as a Star on our journey to deeper faith and understanding. Help us to become sceptres of Your Word. Amen.

The Rock of My Salvation

"The Lord liveth; and blessed be my rock; and exalted be the God of the rock of my salvation." 2 SAMUEL 22:47

No graver danger threatens the believer than forgetting that he or she was redeemed, what his salvation cost, and what the rock foundation of the Christian faith is. To meet this need, our Savior pictures Himself not merely as the Rock of Ages, and our strong Rock of Refuge, but the *Rock of our Salvation*. Here, in Him and upon His merit and atoning grace, we were saved from among the lost. Let us glory in His precious name and never forget that He was "wounded for our transgressions" and "that He bore our sins in His own body on the tree."

Heavenly Father, You are the Rock of our Salvation, the one refuge in a world filled with conflict. Shelter us in Your arms forever. Amen.

King of Glory

*"Who is this King of glory? The Lord of hosts,
he is the King of glory."* PSALM 24:10

Jehovah Jesus, the glorious King! Not merely a king, but glorious, excelling all others in mighty truth and power, grace and love. We almost forget for a time His absolute sovereignty as we bow in humble worship before His matchless glory and cry again and again, "Thy Kingdom come, oh glorious King."

As we look to the day when You come in glory, help us to live humble lives in obeisance to You. Amen.

Wisdom

"I wisdom dwell with prudence, and find out knowledge of witty inventions." PROVERBS 8:12

Wisdom is the right use of knowledge. What a wondrous name for Him who gave Himself for us! Who, "when He putteth forth His own sheep, he goeth before them"; who guides us by the skillfulness of His hand.

May we seek with all our hearts until we find You, and finding You, find wisdom to do the will of God. Amen.

Excellent

*"Let them praise the name of the Lord: for his name
alone is excellent; his glory is above the earth
and heaven."* PSALM 148:13

All the glory of the Lord is that in which He excels all others. His name is Excellent, and all His names that represent some feature of His grace are glorious because they excel any other name ever uttered among men and women. What friend, what helper, do we know on earth who can approach His excellence? And so we turn with new joy to the Psalmist's testimony, "They that know thy name will put their trust in thee."

*Only Your Name is Excellent, oh Lord, and You offer the only
way to salvation. Help us to magnify Your Name. Amen.*

Understanding

*"Counsel is mine, and sound wisdom: I am understanding;
I have strength."* PROVERBS 8:14

God is Love, God is Light, God is to us a thousand things
for which we long and which we need, but have we realized
that in possessing Him and abiding in Him, He is understanding? All that seems dark and difficult will become clear
to us as we depend on Him who is understanding. It would
take ten thousand years to learn a few of the many things we
long to know on earth. The soul that is linked to God begins
to understand and will go on to clearer understanding
throughout the countless ages.

*Dear Heavenly Father, Your understanding has drawn us to You
and binds us ever closer as we study Your Word. We praise Your
holy Name! Amen.*

Jehovah of Hosts

"And one cried unto another, and said, Holy,
holy, holy, is Jehovah of hosts: the whole earth is full
of his glory." ISAIAH 6:3 (RV)

The Jehovah of the Old Testament is the Jesus of the New. If we always think, as Scofield suggested, of Jehovah as "God revealing Himself," and the words of Jehovah—Jesus—as "Blessed are the pure in heart: for they shall see God," then shall the heavens always be full of the chariots and horsemen of Jehovah of hosts. All fear shall be stilled and His revelation of Himself to us will not be in vain.

Lord Jesus, Jehovah of hosts, give us a vision of Your glory this
day. Amen.

A Sanctuary

"And he shall be for a sanctuary...." ISAIAH 8:14

Where is your place of worship? Where in the turmoil of the street, in the busy cares of home, in the hurry and confusion of life shall our souls find the place to pray? "He shall be for a sanctuary, closer to thee than breathing, nearer than hands or feet." At any moment during the hurried day, you may be hidden from all earth's eyes and spared earth's din. Only abide in Him.

Help us to seek You in the quiet moments of a clanging world, oh Lord who is our Sanctuary. Amen.

Wonderful

"For unto us a child is born, unto us a son is given:…and his name shall be called Wonderful." ISAIAH 9:6

Jesus is the same yesterday, today, and forever, and men and women who think Him commonplace, or at most only an unusual man, will sometimes stand ashamed and confounded as they hear this prophecy fulfilled. "His name shall be called Wonderful." In this day, He is working just as wonderful works as when He created the heavens and the earth. His wondrous grace, His wonderful omnipotence, is for His child who needs Him and who trusts Him. Attempt great things for God and expect great things from Him, and you will begin even now to say, His name is Wonderful.

Your wonderful grace and power brings us to our knees. Help us get up and out, sharing Your Good News. Amen.

Counsellor

"For unto us a child is born, unto us a son is given:…and his name shall be called…Counsellor." ISAIAH 9:6

Not often is He called Counsellor now. Conference after conference is held by both the world and the church to find by human wisdom some better plan for earthly government, or for the church, or for the welfare of our earthly life and walk. But how rarely do we bow together or alone to seek that heavenly wisdom, that divine counsel, which alone will enable us to find our way through life's mazes? When will His name be joyfully and triumphantly proclaimed as Counsellor by His people? By you?

Dear Lord and Counsellor, we commit all of life's decisions to you and lay all burdens at Your feet. In everything we seek Your will. Amen.

The Mighty God

"For unto us a child is born, unto us a son is given:...and his name shall be called...The mighty God." ISAIAH 9:6

Have we doubted His might and feared the day when some opponent was near? Focus now on these words: His name is The mighty God. Away with all doubts and fears! "Thou hast made both the heavens and earth. There is nothing too hard for Thee."

Lord, I bow to the dust and worship. Mighty God, show Your power in me! Amen.

The Everlasting Father

*"For unto us a child is born, unto us a son
is given:...and his name shall be called...
The everlasting Father."* ISAIAH 9:6

W ho has not mourned a father's death and felt the loss of his transient power and helpfulness? The Child who was born in Bethlehem, who gave His life for you, is not only your Savior and King but "His name shall be called...The everlasting Father." In His everlasting love, within His ever-lasting arms, within His Father-heart that has infinite compassion, you will find safety, rest, and comfort."

Everlasting Father, we thank You for claiming us as Your children. What an eternal blessing! Amen.

The Prince of Peace

"For unto us a child is born, unto us a son is given:…and his name shall be called…The Prince of Peace." ISAIAH 9:6

My "peace I leave with you, my peace I give unto you; not as the world giveth, give I to you." He who proclaimed these words is rightly called The Prince of Peace. Such peace He brought to earth was, however, rejected by men and our Prince of Peace waits still to be crowned on earth. But He gives before that royal day a peace that passes understanding to every trusting heart. Have you, in loyalty to The Prince of Peace, accepted in humble faith His peace?

While the world offers no lasting peace to our weary souls, we turn to You, our Savior and Prince of Peace, and know You will not reject us. Amen.

The Root of Jesse

"And in that day there shall be a root of Jesse…
to it shall the Gentiles seek: and his rest shall
be glorious." ISAIAH 11:10

It is not Israel alone who shall rejoice when "a root of Jesse shall stand for an ensign of the people." Indeed, "to it shall the Gentiles seek," and all the gracious promises and gifts God gave to Jesse and to David and his seed belong to us who worship Jesus, David's Son and Jesse's Root. How the grace and glory of our God through all the ages is gathered up for us who from the Gentile world bow at His feet and find His glorious rest!

Dear God, Root of Jesse, we thank You for all prophecies fulfilled and those to be realized one day when Your kingdom shall come. Amen.

Strength to the Poor and Needy

"For thou hast been a strength to the poor, a strength to the needy in his distress...." ISAIAH 25:4

Touched with the feeling of our infirmities, our Lord in His omnipotence becomes a strength to the poor and needy. Let us never forget that His strength is made perfect in our weakness only when we realize our helplessness and fling ourselves, as trusting children, into the outstretched arms by which He created the heavens and the earth. With what wondrous picture does our Lord reveal Himself as the supply for our every need and "strength to the poor!"

Let us never forget Your earthly miracles to help the poor and needy. Let us never forget You are always with us. Amen.

A Sure Foundation

"Therefore thus saith the Lord God, Behold, I lay in Zion…a sure foundation: he that believeth shall not make haste." ISAIAH 28:16

All the chiseling, all the polishing of experiences through which we pass is costly. Will it last? Is it worthwhile? Worthwhile to suffer and say, "Dear Lord, stay not thine hand to comfort us and steady us." Through just such testing times the Master calls Himself a sure foundation. No experiment here, no doubt, no room for anxious thought or fear. He who builds upon that sure foundation finds his building sure, and he shall be a pillar in the temple of God to go no more out forever.

We rest on You, our Sure Foundation, knowing one day we will meet in eternity. Amen.

Our Lawgiver

"For the Lord is our judge, the Lord is our lawgiver, the Lord is our king; he will save us." ISAIAH 33:22

Every nation, every act, every life, needs a law to direct it in its relation to its own expression and to others. That law must be made by one who knows and understands the nation, act, or life. Jesus is our lawgiver. He who gave us life, He who has lived the life we need to live, He knows. He made the law for us in infinite tenderness and love. "He that hath my commandments, and keepeth them, he it is that loveth me."

Oh, Lord and Savior, help us to lead lives pleasing to You. Amen.

The Redeemer

"And the Redeemer shall come to Zion, and unto them that turn from transgression in Jacob, saith the Lord." ISAIAH 59:20

When failure comes and disappointment, when your soul has been defeated and the race seems hopeless, stop and think thy Lord redeemed thee and at countless cost. If He saw in you that for which to pay His life, Himself, His all, is it not worthwhile to rise and try again, walking with Him and worshiping Him who redeemed you?

When we consider Your ultimate sacrifice on the cross, help us to find strength to rededicate our lives to You, oh Redeemer. Amen.

Ancient of Days

"I saw in the night visions, and behold, one like the Son of man came with the clouds of heaven, and came to the Ancient of days, and they brought him near before him…his dominion is an everlasting dominion, which shall not pass away, and his kingdom that which shall not be destroyed." DANIEL 7:13,14

"In the beginning was the Word," and He who redeemed us is "the Ancient of days," whose head is "white as snow" (Revelation 1:14). He is from everlasting and will be unto the ages of ages our eternal God. Shall not we, whose lives upon the earth are but a handbreadth, bow in worship and adoration at the feet of the Ancient of days?

Our Lord, who has been and will be forever, we marvel at Your wisdom and are awestruck in Your presence. Amen.

The Branch

"And speak unto him, saying, Thus speaketh the Lord of hosts, saying, Behold the man whose name is The BRANCH; and he shall grow up out of his place, and he shall build the temple of the Lord." ZECHARIAH 6:12

While He was here on earth The Branch said, "The Son can do nothing of Himself, but what he seeth the Father do," taking the place of humility in His utter dependence upon God the Father. Are we tempted to exalt ourselves, to work in some strength that He has given in the past? Let us bow at His feet and remember that except "ye abide in…me ye can do…nothing." Let us consider Him who, although He was the Mighty God, yet called Himself in His earthly relationship The Branch.

We acknowledge that we are helpless lest we cling to The Branch of life, the Source of all power and knowledge. Strengthen our feeble faith, we pray. Amen.

The Messenger of the Covenant

*"Behold, I will send my messenger…even the messenger
of the covenant, whom ye delight in: behold, he shall
come, saith the Lord of hosts."* MALACHI 3:1

He who is our example that we should walk in His steps has
called Himself the messenger of the covenant. The Father
gave a promise to those who should believe in His Son. The
Son came bringing that promise, that covenant, from heaven.
To the true believer that most precious covenant is this: "I will
put my laws into their hearts, and in their minds will I write
them." Will you accept the messenger? "Open thy mouth
wide, and I will fill it."

*Dear Heavenly Father, thank You for sending Your most precious
Son in whom all promises are fulfilled. Amen.*

Son of Abraham

"The book of the generation of Jesus Christ, the son of David, the son of Abraham." MATTHEW 1:1

Three titles in one verse are given: Jesus Christ, Son of David, Son of Abraham. Abraham was the head of the covenant nation. God had given to him the promise that in His seed all the nations of the earth would be blessed. Jesus submitted to the Jewish law in righteousness. He lived as a Jew, He preached to the Jews. And He died for the Jews as well as for all people. "So then they which be of faith are blessed with faithful Abraham" (Galatians 3:9). How wonderful! God manifested in the flesh as Abraham's seed and yet the One who made the promise to Abraham!

Our Savior, You are the promised Son of Abraham and Son of God. Hold us fast in faith in Your Word. Amen.

Jesus

"...Thou shalt call his name JESUS: for he shall save his people from their sins." MATTHEW 1:21

Over seven hundred times in the New Testament the name Jesus (Joshua) is used. How familiar we are with that name! Joshua of the Old Testament saved Israel by leading the people through the River Jordan, fought their battles, and was steadfast in his allegiance to God and His people. Our Lord is our Joshua, One who fights our battles for us, who is our leader, our protector, our Savior! His lordship will never cease until He has us safely in the sheepfold on the other side. Hallelujah, what a Savior!

Savior of our souls, in whom we are separated for eternity, guide us by Your Holy Spirit to the praise of Your grace. Amen.

Emmanuel

"Behold, a virgin…shall bring forth a son, and they shall call his name Emmanuel, which being interpreted is, God with us." MATTHEW 1:23

This was the prophecy of Isaiah 7:14: "Therefore the Lord himself shall give you a sign; Behold, a virgin shall conceive, and bear a son, and shall call his name Immanuel." What a wonderful God and Savior He is, and He is with us as He promised in Matthew 28:19,20: "Go ye therefore, and teach all nations, baptizing them in the name of the Father, and of the Son, and of the Holy Ghost: Teaching them to observe all things whatsoever I have commanded you; and, lo, I am with you alway, even unto the end of the world." Let us sense His presence and make Him real. Walk, talk, live with, and love Him more and more as the days go by.

Lord Jesus, we know that You dwell in us. May we enjoy Your fellowship evermore. Amen.

A Governor

"And thou Bethlehem…for out of thee shall come a Governor, that shall rule my people Israel." MATTHEW 2:6

Bethlehem of Judaea! A little village, twice highly honored! The birthplace of David, king of Israel, and the birthplace of Jesus the Christ, King of kings and Lord of lords! Who could visit this land of promise and not desire to see this city of cities, the place where Jehovah enthroned in human form and lying in a manger gazed into the face of the virgin Mary, His earthly mother. The government shall be upon His shoulders, and He will reign in righteousness. Blessed day!

Dear Lord, our Governor, we pray for Your soon coming, and ask for grace that we may hasten it. Amen.

A Nazarene

"And he came and dwelt in a city called Nazareth: that it might be fulfilled which was spoken by the prophets, He shall be called a Nazarene." MATTHEW 2:23

Nazareth was a town on the northern border of the plain of Esdraelon. To this place came the angel Gabriel, announcing to Mary the coming birth of Christ: "And the angel came in unto her, and said, Hail, thou that art highly favoured, the Lord is with thee: blessed art thou among women" (Luke 1:28). On the night of His betrayal our Lord asked the question, "Whom seek ye?" They replied, "Jesus of Nazareth," and He said, "I am he."

Jesus of Nazareth, may we never be ashamed to be called the followers of the lowly Nazarene. Amen.

Friend of Sinners

"Behold,…a friend of publicans and sinners."
MATTHEW 11:19

These are the words of Jesus Himself. He quotes the phrases of others as applied to Himself. What a title! How wonderfully true it is, a Friend of sinners! So He was, and so He is, a Friend that "sticketh closer than a brother." Laying aside the royal robes of heaven, He came here to befriend sinful men and women. It was a life work that cost Jesus Christ His life. Hallelujah! What a Friend! How gladly He paid the price of friendship. As we take up our life's work, let us ask ourselves the question, "Am I a friend of sinners?" If not, then I am not like my Lord, for He was, and He found joy in it.

Lord Jesus, the world is full of friendless sinners. May we make them acquainted with You, the Friend of sinners. Amen.

Master

*"…For one is your Master, even Christ; and all
ye are brethren."* MATTHEW 23:8

Master here means teacher or leader. The admonition is to
avoid the desire for personal distinction so common among
God's leaders. Let our eyes be fixed upon Him and depend
upon the Holy Spirit who represents Him and who guides us
into all truth (John 16: 13,14). The more we seek to exalt
Him, the less we will think of magnifying ourselves. Make
Him Master of your life, remembering that "the disciple is
not above his master; but everyone that is perfect shall be as
his master" (Luke 6:40). Oh, that we may be as our Master,
the meek and lowly One!

*Our Lord, we need great grace as we seek to follow You as
Master. Amen.*

The Bridegroom

"And while they went to buy, the bridegroom came; and they that were ready went in with him to the marriage: and the door was shut.... Watch therefore, for ye know neither the day nor the hour wherein the Son of man cometh." MATTHEW 25:10, 13

The Bridegroom must come. The true church is His beloved, espoused bride. He has waited a long time for her to prepare herself for the glad day and to add the last believer that will complete the body. Are you thinking of Him as the Coming One? And of yourself as one who is to be blessed as His beloved throughout eternity? How insignificant are all the little cares and trials! How small they seem when our eyes are turned with expectancy toward Him as He comes in the clouds. "Blessed are they which are called unto the marriage supper of the Lamb" (Revelation 19:9). Hallelujah!

Dear Lord, help our faith to grow and give us the confidence to share the Good News with others. In so doing, we will hasten Your blessed return. Amen.

The Holy One of God

"I know thee who thou art, the Holy One of God."
MARK 1:24

What a testimony coming from the lips of one possessed of an unclean spirit, Satan's tool, under his power. But the presence of Christ completely awed him. "I know thee who thou art, the Holy One of God." This was not a willing testimony but was forced from him. Many men and women are devil possessed, and the devil has powers accorded him, but Christ can hinder Satan's followers, can cast out his demons and forbid their speaking. How lovingly we should bow at His feet, the Holy One of God!

Holy One of God, may we fix our thoughts on You and may You glorify Yourself through us. Amen.

Son of Man

"The Son of man shall be delivered unto the chief priests, and unto the scribes; and they shall condemn him to death…." MARK 10:33

In the ninth chapter Jesus had said, "The Son of man is delivered into the hands of men and they shall kill him." How earnestly He sought to stress His approaching sacrifice upon His disciples and how He longed for their sympathy! But, alas, how hard is the human heart. How difficult it is for Jesus to win us to Himself! "The Son of man must suffer many things," He had said, but the saddest of all was the failure of His own beloved disciples to enter into the burden He bore as He approached the cross.

Oh, Holy Son of Man, give unto us the loving hearts that will enter into fellowship with You in all things. Amen.

A Ransom

"For even the Son of man came not to be ministered unto, but to minister, and to give his life a ransom for many."
MARK 10:45

A ransom for many! Here Christ is set forth as the penalty paid for the sins of the world. He took our place as sinners under the judgment wrath of God and paid the penalty and the price of our deliverance with His own blood. Listen to the drops of blood as they fall from His hands and feet and wounded side. They voice the words, "the ransom price for their sins and for the sins of the whole world." Would that men and women everywhere would believe and receive. How dear, how precious is He to us, washed clean in His blood and freed forever from the punishment due us.

Lord, may our ransomed souls well up in praise to Your glorious Name! Amen.

The Word

"In the beginning was the Word, and the Word was with God, and the Word was God." JOHN 1:1

In John's Gospel we find many titles for the Son of God. The book of Genesis commences with creation, but John commences with the Creator. What a foundation for our faith when we know that Jesus was the Word and the Word was God. If we face this tremendous fact, we can feel the throbbing of our hearts and hear a voice that says, "God!" As we look upon the heavens and the clouds, we think "God!" The sun, the moon, the trees, the flowers, and all living creatures seem to shout "God!" Without Him there is nothing. With Him all things are possible!

Oh, our Living Word, who has given us the written Word, help us to abide in You. Amen.

The Lamb of God

"The next day John seeth Jesus coming unto him, and saith, Behold the Lamb of God, which taketh away the sin of the world." JOHN 1:29

Jesus Christ—the Lamb of God—has taken away sin by bearing it. He bore all sin away when He paid the penalty on the cross and shed His atoning blood. God's Lamb! No one else could be God's Lamb. Jesus was the voluntary offering. What can we do? We can believe it, accept it, and take our place with Him.

Let us behold You every day, Jesus, Lamb of God, counting nothing too good to give to You or too much to do for Your Kingdom. Amen.

The Son of God

"And I saw, and bare record that this is the Son of God."
JOHN 1:34

John had not known Jesus as the Messiah although he did know Him to be Mary's son. But when the Holy Spirit descended upon Jesus at His baptism, John knew Him as the Son of God and bore record to the fact. The testimony of John the Baptist is clear: Jesus is God's Son. He is the Promised One. Not *a* Son of God, as some learned critics say condescendingly, but *the* Son of God. We should seek to be like John the Baptist, or a signpost pointing to Him and saying, "Behold! the Son of God." John laid down his life for his loyalty to the Son of God. May we be willing to suffer anything so that our testimony shall be clear and clean always for Him.

Lord, help us to bring someone to know You. Amen.

Rabbi

"Nathanael answered and saith unto him, Rabbi, thou art the Son of God; thou art the King of Israel." JOHN 1:49

Rabbi means teacher and is used seven times in the New Testament. Nathanael recognized Christ as a teacher, and He was, without doubt, the greatest Teacher that ever lived. A careful study of the four Gospels with a view to learning how Christ taught, His method, His manner, and His purpose, is better than any other training for Bible teachers. Christ was a true teacher. He taught the truth. He spoke to men and women of low estate. He used words that were easily understood. He illustrated His messages in a practical manner. "The common people heard Him gladly." That was a high compliment indeed.

Lord, help us to teach by our lips and by our lives. We pray that we may so teach by Your example. Amen.

His Only Begotten Son

> *"For God so loved the world, that he gave his only begotten Son, that whosoever believeth in him should not perish, but have everlasting life."* JOHN 3:16

Here is the most beloved verse in the Bible. What a revelation of God, of Christ, of the depths and power of love! How could He? Abraham gave his son, and God graciously gave him back. But God's Son—the Son of His love—the Only Begotten One—was given to a lost world, to sinful men and women. How did He give Him? Clothed in human form, a Man! Oh, the wonders of such a love! How this act should stir our hearts! How we should love God for His gift! How we should love our Lord Jesus Christ, God's Only Begotten Son!

Let us with undying enthusiasm for a lost world go forth to tell the story to a sinful world. Amen.

Messiah

*"The woman saith unto him, I know that
Messiah cometh, which is called Christ: when he is
come, he will tell us all things."*
JOHN 4:25

There is no book like the Bible and there never can be. Christ's interview with the woman at the well and His revelation of Himself is unique and contrary to any conception that could have been made of Him. The Samaritans, as did the Jews, anticipated a Christ (an Anointed One). This was the promise given in Deuteronomy 18:18. This woman was the last one we would have chosen for such a revelation, but her soul was filled at once with the Spirit of life and hope. Her lips bore a testimony, humiliating to herself, but bringing salvation to a multitude. Oh, that our lips might bear such convincing, convicting, and converting testimony.

Lord, make us like this Samaritan woman! Amen.

The Christ, the Savior of the World

"For we have heard him ourselves, and know that this is indeed the Christ, the Saviour of the world." JOHN 4:42

The testimony of one woman brings forth from the lips of many this title, Christ, the Savior of the world. For a two-day revival, Christ tarried in the little city of the Samaritans and there was a blessed first fruit of His glory. These people, unlike the Jews, asked for no signs or miracles. They took Him at His Word, just as we must do. When He speaks, it is God that speaks. "We have heard him ourselves." The need of the world today is the personal experience of believers manifested in a personal devotion to Christ and in personal testimony to a spiritually hungry world.

Oh, Christ, Savior of the world, baptize us with the Spirit of service for You. Amen.

The Living Bread

"I am the living bread which came down from heaven: if any man eat of this bread, he shall live for ever: and the bread that I will give is my flesh, which I will give for the life of the world." JOHN 6:51

Jesus tells us that He will lay down His own life in order that we may have this living bread to eat and so live forever. The process by which we are to nourish the new nature that we received by accepting Him is by feeding on Him. If our bodies do not assimilate food, they perish; in the proportion that we do assimilate our food, we are able bodied. Here is a searching lesson: Many believers are not strong. Paul says, "For this cause many are weak and sickly among you and many sleep."

Lord, make us strong through feeding on You. Amen.

The Light of the World

"Then spake Jesus unto them again, saying, I am the light of the world: he that followeth me shall not walk in darkness, but shall have the light of life." JOHN 8:12

And God said, "Let there be light; and there was light." And "God divided the light from the darkness." Now our Lord says, "I am the light of the world." The world is a dark, gloomy place, but "God is light and in him is no darkness at all." If we follow Him we shall not walk in darkness. "If we walk in the light," we have fellowship with one another and reflect the glory of His person in the gloom of the world. "Arise, shine; for thy light is come, and the glory of the Lord is risen upon thee." He can only be manifested through the lives of His own and the light of the Word.

Oh, Lord of light, shine in our hearts and through our lives. Amen.

I AM

"Jesus said unto them, Verily, verily, I say unto you, Before Abraham was, I am." JOHN 8:58

The life of Abraham was limited. We know the time of his birth and of his departure. But there is no time limit to the life of our Lord. "Before Abraham was, I am." He was the eternal Son of God. He was the Uncreated One, the Eternal One, the Self-existent One. Before the creation of the world He was the "I AM." After the world passes away He will still be the "I AM." Without Him nothing was made that was made. He was God! Wonder of wonders, God manifest in the flesh! God pleading with men, God on the cross, God in the glory and coming in the clouds! Great is the mystery of God!

Son of God, Son of man, at the right hand of the Glory, we bow in Your presence and say with deepest reverence, "Hallowed be thy name." Amen.

The Good Shepherd

"I am the good shepherd: the good shepherd giveth his life for the sheep." JOHN 10:11

God is good, and Jesus is God. Therefore, He is good. If we could stop for a few moments and sense His presence, longing to speak to us in tones of deepest love, with His wonderful eyes fixed upon us, and His holy desire to draw us in loving tenderness to Himself, we would say, "He is so good, He died for me." Surely our hearts would go out in passionate love to Him," the Good Shepherd.

Loving Shepherd, help us to keep close to You and not to stray from Your fold. Amen.

The Resurrection

"Jesus said unto her, I am the resurrection, and the life: he that believeth in me, though he were dead, yet shall he live." JOHN 11:25

Here our Lord links His own title of I AM with the Resurrection. Faith in Him equals eternal life and that assures our resurrection. Because He lives, we *must* live. Death may come to us, but it will be the shadow only, which will pass and leave us in the full sunlight of eternal life. Nothing can separate us from our Lord. He who raised up Christ from the dead shall quicken our bodies. "Whosoever liveth and believeth in me, shall never die." In His Resurrection He conquered death. Praise the Lord!

Lord Jesus, come quickly and change these bodies of our abasement into the likeness of Your own glorified body. Amen.

A Grain of Wheat

"And Jesus answered them, saying, The hour is come, that the Son of man should be glorified. Verily, verily, I say unto you, Except a corn [grain] of wheat fall into the ground and die, it abideth alone: but if it die, it bringeth forth much fruit."
JOHN 12:23, 24

Before Jesus could be glorified He must be as a grain of wheat. How insignificant seems a grain of wheat, and yet this suggestion is one of the most wonderful in the Word of God. A grain of wheat is so small that it can hardly be held between the fingers, and yet it is associated with *His glory*. He must die in order to bring forth fruit. So must we, if we are to be like Him. How hard it seems to human pride to become as a grain of wheat and then to die to this world. But listen to the words of His testimony and look upon His example. Do we desire to be like Him?

Lord, help us to ponder this truth and long to be more like You. Amen.

The Man

"Then came Jesus forth, wearing the crown of thorns, and the purple robe. And Pilate saith unto them, Behold the man!" JOHN 19:5

"Behold the man!" How little Pilate knew what he was doing when he bestowed upon our Lord that significant title. The word man is used nearly three thousand times in the Bible, but there is only one "the man," the Man from heaven. The word in the original text is "Adam"—a human being— and so He was. It seems too good to be true, and yet it is true. For our sakes—in order to be one with us and to bear our sin—He threw aside His royal vesture and donned the garments of humanity, that He might interpret to us the purpose of the Father.

In the name of this Man, our Father, we ask for guidance and pray that our hearts may be in tune with His. Amen.

The Lord

"For whosoever shall call upon the name of the Lord shall be saved." ROMANS 10:13

The Master loves to hear the call of a sinner for salvation. How many sin-plagued, weary souls there are who are hungry for salvation. They do not know this verse. They have false ideas about Christ and about salvation. They would gladly cry to the Lord but He has not been revealed to them. They need someone to tell them of His longing to have them in His family. "Faith cometh by hearing and hearing by the Word of God." Listen to these words: "How beautiful are the feet of them that preach the Gospel of peace, and bring glad tidings of good things!" To preach means to tell out or to proclaim, and if you are a believer, you are a God-ordained preacher and will be held accountable for your ministry.

Oh, Lord, our Master, send us out to tell the love story to others. Amen.

The Deliverer

*"And so all Israel shall be saved: as it is written,
There shall come out of Sion the Deliverer, and shall
turn away ungodliness from Jacob."* ROMANS 11:26

Here we face a startling prophecy. The ancient people of God, scattered about in every land without a country of their own, save as certain permission is given them to reside in the old land, are to be delivered and as a nation turn to Christ as their Deliverer. They shall be God's earthly people as we shall be His heavenly people. Let us never forget how much we owe to the Jewish race and let us seek earnestly to bring as many as possible to Christ.

Oh, Lord Jesus, You are our Deliverer. We glory in Your name. Help us to help others to know You. Amen.

Creator of All Things

"For by him were all things created, that are in heaven, and that are in earth, visible and invisible, whether they be thrones, or dominions, or principalities, or powers: all things were created by him, and for him." COLOSSIANS 1:16

He is the Creator of all things, visible and invisible! Do not allow the magnitude of this revelation to escape you. Are we not prone to underestimate Him and undervalue His work? See how Paul visualizes it in Ephesians 3:8,9: "Unto me, who am less than the least of all saints, is this grace given, that I should preach among the Gentiles the unsearchable riches of Christ; And to make all men see what is the fellowship of the mystery, which from the beginning of the world hath been hid in God, who created all things by Jesus Christ." Should we not take a place lower than Paul who counted himself the least of all saints?

Lord, help us. Keep ambition and pride from dominating us. Keep us at Your feet in worship and praise. Amen.

Lord of Peace

*"Now the Lord of peace himself give you peace
always by all means. The Lord be with you all."*
2 THESSALONIANS 3:16

Our Lord is the Author of peace. He came to make peace
possible. "Peace I leave with you; my peace I give unto you."
In order to have this wonderful peace we must be yoked to
Him. We live in a world of unrest and conflict. The heart of
humanity beats high with excitement. "No peace for the
wicked!" How we should reach out to them! They do not
know Him. They can never know Him unless He is revealed
to them. We are His spokespeople. Let us cheerfully make
Him manifest.

*Lord of Peace, we pillow our heads on Your chest. Your peace
truly surpasses understanding. We thank You. Amen.*

The Righteous Judge

"Henceforth there is laid up for me a crown of righteousness, which the Lord, the righteous judge, shall give me at that day: and not to me only, but unto all them also that love his appearing." 2 TIMOTHY 4:8

In the judgment spoken of here, there is a promised reward that Paul says will come to himself and to all who love the truth concerning the coming of the Lord. These believers are to be crowned and the Lord Himself will put the crown upon their heads: "a crown of righteousness." There are many crowns awaiting the saints. Salvation is a *gift*, but crowns are for those whose lives have been lived in obedience to the Word of God. His shed blood should be the appeal to us to be willing to lay down our lives for Him.

Lord Jesus, give us an increasing desire to see and be with You. Help us to complete the Body and thus hasten Your coming. Amen.

Heir of All Things

*"Hath in these last days spoken unto us by his Son,
whom he hath appointed heir of all things, by
whom also he made the worlds."* HEBREWS 1:2

How logical the Bible is. To our Lord is ascribed glory because He is the Creator of all things. He made the worlds. He says, "All things that the Father hath are mine." Unlimited power is His. Unlimited possessions are His. We are also His. Praise God, what a revelation we have of Him! He purchased us with His own precious blood. We are dear to Him; we are the apple of His eye. He will never leave us nor forsake us. We belong to the "heir of all things." Our needs will be supplied, then, for we are heirs of God and joint-heirs with Jesus Christ. Let us keep our heads erect and our eyes turned heavenward.

Oh blessed heir of all things, take us under Your wings and may we be gloriously happy in fellowship with You. Amen.

The High Priest

"...Consider...the High Priest of our profession, Christ Jesus." HEBREWS 3:1

We are called here as "holy brethren" to consider Jesus Christ as High Priest. We cannot be called upon too often to consider Him as our High Priest seeing that "He ever liveth to make intercession for us." Could we make it our life habit to, every morning, spend a few moments in contemplation of Him as *our* High Priest, and take up life's duties with that picture before us, seeing Him clothed in the garments of the High Priest, in the Holy of Holies, we would be better believers.

May our eyes be upon You, our great High Priest. Amen.

The Author of Our Faith

"Looking unto Jesus, the author and finisher of our faith." HEBREWS 12:2

The Author or leader of our faith is Jesus. Look to Him, for the inspiration to faith is found in Him. He is the prophesied and promised "seed of the woman" bruised by Satan. He paid the penalty and then robbed the grave of its power, rose in the majesty of His glorified body, and will come someday to bruise the serpent's (Satan's) head, and will master and imprison him. He inspires us by His sacrificial death and by His precious promises. His message is "Follow me. I will never leave thee nor forsake thee." And our response to Him should be, "Lead on; we will follow You even unto death."

Oh, great Author of our Faith, with unwavering faith may we follow You to the end. Amen.

My Helper

"So that we may boldly say, The Lord is my helper, and I will not fear what man shall do unto me." HEBREWS 13:6

What a difference there is in believers! How timid some are. Is it because they do not know the promises? "The fear of man bringeth a snare; but whoso putteth his trust in the Lord shall be safe." And consider this passage: "The angel of the Lord encampeth round about them that fear him, and delivereth them." Courage of conviction is the crying need of the Christian today, conviction based on God's Holy Word and God's call to service. He has said, "I will never leave thee, nor forsake thee." Faith takes hold upon this promise and allows nothing to move it.

Lord Jesus, our Helper, help us to lean hard upon Your gracious promises and have a joyful life. Amen.

The Advocate

"My little children, these things write I unto you, that ye sin not. And if any man sin, we have an advocate with the Father, Jesus Christ the righteous." 1 JOHN 2:1

Sin is the existing nature of humanity. God, in love, has recognized the needs of men and women and has made provisions. We sin when we "come short of the glory of God." So Christ became our Advocate, or "one who comes alongside," to stand by us. When Satan charges us with sin, Christ represents us and defends us. He is the attorney who handles our case. His propitiation (or covering for sin) is manifested in all His work for us: in His life, His death, His Resurrection, His ascension, and His intercession.

Lord, we thank You that You appear for us and through You we are all accepted by our Heavenly Father. Amen.

The Faithful Witness

"…Jesus Christ, who is the faithful witness…."
REVELATION 1:5

This was the testimony of Christ Himself when He stood before Pilate (John 18:37): "To this end was I born, and for this cause came I into the world, that I should bear witness unto the truth. Everyone that is of the truth heareth my voice." This was His mission, to bear faithful witness. This is the obligation of every believer, "ye shall be witnesses unto me." This is the failure in a large measure of the church. The unsaved are waiting for the testimony by lip and life of professing Christians, and, as they behold it, they are convicted by the Holy Spirit.

May the Holy Spirit Himself so control our lives that we shall count it our highest privilege to manifest Him before a world consumed with denial. Amen.

The Alpha and Omega

"I am Alpha and Omega, the beginning and the ending, saith the Lord, which is, and which was, and which is to come, the Almighty." REVELATION 1:8

As alpha is the first letter of the Greek alphabet and omega is the last, so our Lord is first and last. He is the Source of all things. He is the Source of all truth, of all the promises given in the Word of God, of all the prophecies, of all commands, and of all penalties. How great is our Lord, "which is, and which was, and which is to come," the all-inclusive One! Everything is involved in the two words "beginning" and "ending" and one word includes it all—"is."

Oh, Jehovah-Elohim, First and Last, who sees and knows all things, hold us by Your hand. Amen.

The Lion of the Tribe of Judah

"Behold, the Lion of the tribe of Juda[h], the Root of David, hath prevailed to open the book and to loose the seven seals thereof." REVELATION 5:5

The dying prophecy of Jacob was fulfilled in Jesus: "The sceptre shall not depart from Judah, nor a lawgiver from between his feet until Shiloh come" (Genesis 49:10). Jacob had no conception that nearly three thousand years would pass before his prophecy would or could be fulfilled, or that its fulfillment would involve the glorified Son of God. The characteristics of a lion are manifest in the life and work of the Messiah. He will arrest every opposing force of Satan and establish His universal kingdom. Glory be to God, we will be with Him, and we will be like Him in the final overthrow of Satan's kingdom.

Lord, help us to be like You. Help us to wear the armor of warriors and carry the Sword of the Spirit. Amen.

King of Kings

"...And the Lamb shall overcome them: for he is Lord of lords, and King of kings: and they that are with him are called, and chosen, and faithful." REVELATION 17:14

He has upon His garments, and upon His thigh, the name King of kings. Who has? The One born in a manger who found fellowship with fishermen, as He longs for fellowship with us today. A sharp sword issues from His mouth, the Sword of the Spirit, which is the Word of God. As His enemies fell before His presence in the Garden of Gethsemane, so fall they at the end of the world as we know it. The power of God's Word is irresistible. How foolish are they whose feeble hands are raised up against the King of kings, the Mighty One! What judgment awaits all those who oppose Him and His unerring Word!

King of kings, we bow to You. As we follow You, help us to fight the good fight of faith. Amen.